IMAGES
of Wales

CATHAYS, MAINDY
GABALFA AND MYNACHDY

'Then there is another district adjoining Cathays Park, called Cathays. There is nothing of far Cathay, with its fabled wealth, about this quarter, unless it is the sign of the Chinese laundry, for it is a real working class district.' [J. Kyrle Fletcher]

IMAGES
of Wales

CATHAYS, MAINDY
GABALFA AND MYNACHDY

Compiled by
Brian Lee

TEMPUS

First published 1998, reprinted 2000
Copyright © Brian Lee, 1998

Tempus Publishing Limited
The Mill, Brinscombe Port
Stroud, Gloucestershire GL5 2QG

ISBN 0 7524 1030 X

Typesetting and origination by
Tempus Publishing Limited
Printed in Great Britain by
Midway Clark Printing, Wiltshire

This book is dedicated to my grandson, James Lee Harvey

Contents

Acknowledgements

First of all, I would like to thank my wife Jacqueline who not only gave me the idea for this book, but who also acted as my chauffeuse driving me to those people who loaned me their photographs.

Other people I need to thank are Chalford's project editor, Simon Eckley, for giving me the opportunity to compile this book and for helping me with the layout. The editors of the *South Wales Echo* and *Cardiff Post* deserve a big thank you for publishing my requests for photographs in their papers. Without their help this book may never have been published. I need to thank the staff of the Cardiff Central Library local studies department for their assistance and my son-in-law Russell Harvey for helping me transfer the text from my word processor on to his computer. For the loan of photographs, and permission to use them, I am greatly indebted to the following: Paul Keeping, of Cardiff and County Council's Sports and Leisure Department; Cardiff and County Library, especially J. Brynmor Jones; Western Mail & Echo Limited; Wendy Whitfield, Gloria Williams, Eve Daniels, Edna Storror, Marion Jenkins, Barbara Sugarman, Roger Pitman, Richard Britton, Doreen Hobbs, Joan Taylor, Elaine Searle, Glyn Parfitt, Rod Hill, Dennis and Carol Lloyd, Ted and Joan Burnell, Malcolm Meyrick, Jeff Roach, Reta Gale, Margaret Baldwin, Bob Goodall, Geoff North, Vic Wheeler, Valerie Beames, Thelma Davies, Allen Hambly, Mabel Evans, Bernard Baldwin MBE, John Bishop, Mr Stickler, Andrew Williams, Robert Summerhayes, Philip Donovan, Brynley Lawrence, Mrs Beryl Harvey, Mr and Mrs Peter Clifton, Mrs F. Martin, Bill Barrett, John Walsh, Idris John (of the Emporium, Castle Arcade), David Yorath, Marion Dowson, Andrew Williams and Derek Paul (of Now and Then, Crwys Road), and John Billot. I would also like to thank those people who offered photographs which, for one reason or another, were not used and ask forgiveness of any contributors who may have been inadvertently omitted from these acknowledgements.

Brian Lee with his previous book, *Cardiff remembered*

Introduction

In a book of this kind space, or rather lack of it, does not permit us to delve too deeply into the history or origins of the suburbs covered. So let us rely on the old Cardiff County and Borough Records published between 1898 and 1911 to give us a brief description of the origins of the places we will be visiting in the ensuing pages.

Cathays (or 'the Cat Hayes') is the immediate north-eastern suburb of Cardiff. The second part 'hays', we are told, originally stood for an open tract of common land and is also found in other towns; 'cat', meanwhile, is perhaps a corruption of the Welsh 'cad', meaning battle, which may point to the site of a now-forgotten military clash.

Cathays Grange (also known as the Heath Grange or Grange Farm) was an ancient farmhouse and barn on the north-western outskirts of Cathays, towards Llystalybont. Situated at what is now the west end of Llantrisant Street, it may have been the grange for the Manor of Roath-Tewkesbury. (The farm buildings were demolished in 1899 and this book contains some photographs taken in its final years.)

Maindy, or 'Maendy' as it was once known, is described as a farmhouse and hamlet on the North Road, about a mile north of Cardiff, in the manor of Llandaff. The name is said to date from a time when timber or wattle houses were the only ones in the vicinity. There used to be a farm called Maendy Bach, a short distance south of the other farmhouse.

Mynachdy, also known as 'Monachty', was an old farmhouse in the manor of Llandaff and chapelry of Whitchurch, on the site of a pre-Norman religious foundation while Mynachdy Bach was the name of a smaller holding – a thatched house with extensive buildings.

Gabalfa, or 'Caubalfa' as it was then called, was a small village with a mansion in the parish of Llandaff, on the left bank of the River Taff and close to Llandaff ford and bridge. Now it is best known as a large council estate which sprung up in the early 1950s.

Compiling the photographs for this book brought back many happy memories of a boyhood spent in Cathays, Maindy, and Gabalfa. In those days families seemed to live closer together. I had an Aunt Sarah (my father's sister) and an Aunt Eileen (my mother's sister) in the same street. Just around the corner in Wyeverne Road lived my Aunt Elsie, my mother's other sister. Mother, or 'Mama', as my sister Valerie and I called her, like most people, left the house key on a piece of string behind the front door. Visitors could then let themselves in if there was no one in the house! This was in the late 1940s and early 1950s when mother would get down on her knees and scrub the pavement in front of our Thesiger Street house in a sort of half-circle fashion. My maternal grandmother, 'Nana Donovan', moved to Gabalfa from Frederick Street in the 1950s with her son, my uncle Philip and his wife my aunt Mary. This was in the days before television took over our leisure time and I would visit them every Sunday evening. We would play a horse-racing game called 'Escalado' and it brought us many hours of fun and excitement even if we were only playing for a few coppers.

What fun we kids had in the great snowfall of 1947. We built igloos and I can vouch for what they say about them being really warm inside. Heavy rain used to see flooding under the Lowther Road and Salisbury Road bridges. One year a lorry loaded with coal became stuck under Lowther Road Bridge, making the rainwater black. But it did not stop 'Blocko' and the Rhymney Street kids getting out their swimsuits (we called them 'bathers') and having a swim. 'Blocko', I should explain, sold tram blocks for firewood on a hand-cart he pushed through the streets. We used to annoy him by following him and shouting out 'Blocko' and then running for our lives. When the circus came to town the elephants would be stabled at the Park Coal Company yard in Rhymney Street. I recall one sad occasion when one of the company's horses dropped dead in Rhymney Street. People came from neighbouring streets to see the poor creature being hauled by chains on to a waggon.

In this book there are several pictures of Harry Parfitt whose scrap-metal business was in Thesiger Street. His motto was 'Don't Tarry Sell to Harry', and on his horse-drawn cart he would trot through the streets touting for business. For a bundle of rags he would give you a balloon on a stick or a goldfish in a jam jar. The coalman, the baker, and the milkman all delivered their goods then by horse and cart. I remember that the milkman's horse knew the rounds as well as the milkman himself, always stopping and starting at the right houses. Once, outside Cissie's fish and chip shop in Coburn Street, I impersonated his master's voice so well that when I told the horse to 'Gee-up' it actually did. You could always tell the keen gardeners in our street as they would rush out with a bucket and shovel as soon as a horse and cart appeared!

The old Maindy Stadium photographs also hold happy memories for me. As a Roath (Cardiff) Harrier, I trained from there regularly for many years. I ran my first marathon from Maindy Stadium in 1958 and was thrilled to run alongside – even if it was only for a few hundred yards down Allensbank Road! – the 1948 Olympic Games silver medallist, Welshman Tom Richards. However, Tom was nothing like the Olympic athlete I had envisaged. He toed the line wearing a pair of ordinary daps, a tatty vest, and baggy shorts. Tradition had it that Tommy Wood (Newport Harriers) always led the competitors out of the stadium gate into Maindy Road. But nobody had told rookie me! So I came in for some stick. Still, seeing as I was first out and last in I did not do myself any favours. I had a second embarrassing Maindy moment on another occasion. I had just returned from a ten-mile run when the club's star half-miler (he shall remain nameless) wanted to do a 660-yard time trial. However, the athlete he had planned to pace him had not turned up. Although I had just ran ten miles I volunteered to act as his pacemaker. Much to everyone's surprise, including my own, I not only paced him, I beat him! Who can forget Maindy Stadium's sports officer Alf (Mr Maindy) Jensen. A qualified AAA coach, Alf wasn't known for his diplomacy. He treated everyone the same whether they were international athletes or ordinary club runners.

One could go on and on recalling those happy and seemingly carefree days of yesteryear. However, it is time now to let the pictures 'do the talking'. I hope you enjoy looking at them as much as I have.

Brian J. Lee

One
Civic Centre

Workmen put the finishing touches
to the Welsh dragon on the dome
of the City Hall, 1906. The City
Hall was officially opened by the
Marquis of Bute that year.

Children gathered in Cathays Park when King Edward VII and Queen Alexandra visited Cardiff on 13 July 1907 to open Alexandra Dock.

The National Museum of Wales, *c.* 1926. The museum was opened by King George V on 21 April 1927. The eastern wing and the Reardon Smith Lecture Theatre were opened in 1932. The statue depicts Lord Ninian Stuart who had been killed at Loos during the First World War.

The Law Courts, *c.* 1926. These buildings were completed in 1906. They were designed by E.A. Rickards who was also the architect of the City Hall.

Godfrey Charles Morgan, the 1st Viscount Lord Tredegar on his faithful charger, Sir Briggs, *c.* 1920. The statue, by Goscombe John, was unveiled by the Earl of Plymouth in Lord Tredegar's presence on 25 October 1909, the anniversary of the famous Charge of the Light Brigade.

Spillers' Brigade of the British Legion gathers outside the City Hall, *c.* 1920.

GORSEDD GARDENS, CATHAY PARK, CARDIFF.

Gorsedd Gardens, Cathays Park, *c.* 1938. The Gorsedd circle was erected in Cathays Park for the National Eisteddfod of Wales held there in 1899. The circle has been at its present site since 1905 and Gorsedd Gardens was opened to the public in July 1910. *'In front of the National Museum building is a flower garden, and on the green turf is a circle of rough unhewn stones, the Gorsedd Circle of the Bards of the Islands of Britain. It was here that the National Eisteddfod was proclaimed, with the pomp and strange ritual, when it was held in Cardiff.'* [extract from J. Kyrle Fletcher's *Cardiff notes: picturesque and biographical*]

The Welsh National War Memorial, Alexandra Gardens, *c.* 1930. The completed memorial had been unveiled by the Prince of Wales in 1928.

Mrs Jacqueline Lee and her baby daughter Amanda seated in Crown Gardens which was later to become the site of the Welsh Office's car park, *c.* 1961.

Leaving the Welsh National War Memorial in 1953 are, from left to right, Sir Cennydd Traherne, Lady Mayoress Winifred Collins, Field Marshal Montgomery, and the Lord Mayor Sir James Collins.

Prince Charles paid a visit to Cardiff after his investiture as Prince of Wales in 1969.

Two

Trades

The Bon Marché, Woodville Road,
Cathays, 1912.

Woodville Road, Cathays, *c.* 1904. Woodville Road was named after Colonel Edward Robert Wood, the landowner at the time of its construction.

The Flora Hotel, Cathays Terrace, *c.* 1880. This pub was a regular haunt of the author in the 1950s when Horace Brittain played the piano in the upstairs room.

The Royal George Hotel, Crwys Road, *c*. 1891. The area of land near the junction of Crwys Road, City Road, and Albany Road was at one time known as 'the Gallows Field' and it was near here, on 22 July 1679, that Father John Lloyd and Father Phillip Evans were executed for exercising their Catholic, priestly duties. Until recently it was known as Clancy's Irish Bar, but is now known as the George and is said to be haunted by Humphrey, a friendly poltergeist.

The Woodville Hotel, 1891. It is now popularly known to students as the 'Woody'.

The Crwys Hotel, Crwys Road, 1891. Mine host was William J. Lewis.

The Crwys Hotel, a year earlier in 1890. The shop on the right of the picture was run by Robert J. Hollyman the confectioner.

An advertisement for Edward Arnold Ltd which appeared in the St Mark's Church magazine.

Coronet cinema-goers bought their sweets from Yorath's sweet shop on Woodville Road, pictured here c. 1961.

Yorath's grocery stores, Woodville Road, June 1969. From left to right: David Yorath, his mother Mary Ellen, and his wife Nessie. This family store closed in 1984 after trading for fifty years.

Eve and Dave Daniels outside their grocery shop which used to be at No. 148 Malefant Street, Cathays, 1938.

W.G. Parker's grocery store window in Cathays Terrace which won second prize in the 1960 Dairy Festival. The shop was later an ironmonger's and DIY store until it closed in 1999.

Grocer George Parker is seen here, third from the left, standing next to his sister Margaret. In the doorway wearing a hat is their mother Mrs Ethel Parker.

W.G. Parker's grocery store on the occasion of a Weston's Wagon Wheels chocolate biscuit promotion, *c.* 1957. The wagon can be seen to the left of the picture in Minister Street. A Red Indian chief can be spotted in the doorway.

Evans's general store, Coburn Street, Cathays, *c.* 1957. From left to right: Jack Hayes, John Buckley, Jack Goodall, Terry Harvey, Kenny Harris, Bob Goodall, and Malcolm Keenor.

In the 1920s Rumney butcher, Mr Thomas Batten, pictured here third from the right, had three shops in Salisbury Road.

Morris Burnell (left) and Alf Martin who both worked for the Park Coal Company in Rhymney Street, Cathays, *c.* 1950.

It is December 1956 and Cathays Terrace butcher Jack Smith and his assistant, grandson John Creed, show off the Christmas turkeys.

Travelling greengrocer Bill Haynes and Mrs Elvira Evans outside her daughter Mabel's drapers in Coburn Street, Cathays, *c.* 1950.

The Bishops of Cathays had a catering firm as well as a bakery in Harriet Street and both were well known for their meat pies, *c*. 1950.

A familiar sight in the Whitchurch Road area in the 1950s were the vehicles of William England & Sons Dairies. Enjoying a ride on the horse and cart is David Gale.

Brothers Arthur and Glyn Parfitt outside their scrap-metal yard in Thesiger Street, Cathays, c. 1970.

Harry Parfitt shaking hands with Eamon Andrews on the much-loved television show of the 1950s *What's My Line*.

Maud and James Tyler outside their general stores which traded at No. 85 Whitchurch Road from around 1930 to 1960.

The Bon Marché on Crwys Road had ceased trading when this picture was taken in 1982. The author had his first long-trousers suit, costing £5, from here.

Three
Schooldays

Crwys Road School, Cathays, c. 1953. *'I used to go to Crwys Road School, but during the war the army took it over. My sister Beryl and me were then transferred to Albany Road School. I left school at fourteen and went to work in Peacocks in Woodville Road. Next door to where we lived in Thesiger Street was Caton's the dry cleaners later Bollom's. The American soldiers used to take their uniforms to be dry-cleaned there and some of the residents took them in as guests.'* [Edna Storror (née Davey)]

Woodwork class at Crwys Road School, 1919. It closed as an elementary school in 1939 and, later, it became the first home of the College of Food Technology.

Pupils at Crwys Road School, *c.* 1915. A supermarket now stands on the former site of this school.

Crwys Road School and Chapel, *c.* 1890. When this picture was taken the Master was Mr.G. Cook and the Mistress Miss E. Richards. Miss Bale was the infants' mistress and the caretaker was Philip Williams.

Crwys Road School children, *c.* 1901.

Cathays National School, 1945. 'I went to Cathays National which was known, for some reason, as "Jerry's College". We were marched on Ascension Day, St David's Day, and St Andrew's Day to St Andrew's and St Teilo's Church.' [Emrys 'Emmo' Davies]

Class 1A at Cathays National School, 1944. The boy wearing 'wellies' extreme left, is Dennis Giggs, grandfather of Welsh soccer international Ryan Giggs.

Cathays National School baseball team, *c*. 1947. The boy in the centre is Norman Collard who lived in Thesiger Street. To the right of him is Dennis Giggs.

PORTHCAWL CAMP. FEB. 1950.

Cathays National, St Monica's and Viriamu Jones's schools at Porthcawl School Camp, February 1950.

St Cyprian's Sunday school, Bruce Street, *c.* 1946.

St Cyprian's Sunday school, 1920.

34

St Cyprian's Whitsun treat, 1938.

Interior of St Cyprian's Church, 1957.

Pupils at Gladstone School, c. 1908. Opened in 1906, it was named after the nineteenth-century Liberal prime minister, William Ewart Gladstone (1809–98). The building was erected on the former site of a farmhouse called Crwys Bychan, which was demolished in 1899.

Class 3 at Gladstone School, 1934.

Gladstone School, *c.* 1906.

A rather serious-looking six-year-old Roger
Pitman poses for his picture in the Gladstone
School playground, 1950.

Gladstone School pupils group photograph, 1949.

A happy group of Gladstone School infants, *c.* 1965.

Gladstone School junior girls, *c.* 1948. The teacher is Miss Teasal. The girl second left (middle row) is Audrey Martin whose father, Alf Martin is shown on page 23.

Gladstone School girls, 1948.

Dafydd ap Gwilym house athletics team at Cathays High School, 1950.

Cathays High School put on *King Lear* in 1953. The young man at the back of the picture, who played Lear, is Robert Pointon who went on to become a professional actor. Third left back row is David Yorath who played the Duke of Kent.

Prefects at Cathays High School for Girls, 1939.

Viriamu Jones School caretakers Vivian and Winifred Wakeling with their son Ted. *'Before Viriamu Jones School was built in the mid-1920s, there was just a huge field, which stretched back to College Road, and our house, which backed on to the school playground, was the only one in it.'* [Joan Taylor (née Wakeling)]

Viriamu Jones Girls' School, 1932. Joan Taylor (née Wakeling) is second from right in the back row.

Standard 2 at Viriamu Jones Boys' School, *c*. 1933.

Viriamu Jones School, Cefn Road, June 1961. Later this became South Glamorgan Teachers' Centre. It was named after John Viriamu Jones (1856–1901) a well-known educationalist.

Viriamu Jones School, 1933.

Boys at Viriamu Jones School, 1938. Fourth left, middle row, is Viv Brooks, later to become Assistant Chief Constable of South Wales.

Empire Day (24 May) celebrations at Viriamu Jones School, 1932.

St Monica's School on Empire Day, 1936.

St Monica's School, 1940.

Standard 5 at Allensbank Road School, *c. 1923*. The girl circled is Dyllas Roberts.

Pupils at Allensbank Road School, *c. 1956*.

Allensbank Road School children, 20 April 1944.

These children from Cathays having a picnic in Roath Park's Rose Gardens, c. 1938, are from left to right: Ken Parfitt, Pauline Richards, Jean Parfitt, Pamela Davies, Joyce Greenslade, Glyn Parfitt, Valerie Parfitt, Ray Richards, Sharon ?, and Margaret Petheram. Ray Richards went on to become an international cyclist and represented Wales in the 1958 Empire and Commonwealth Games at Cardiff.

Children watching a film show in Florentia Street put on by Mr Idris Jenkins, *c.* 1952. Among those pictured are Glenys Jenkins, Marion Jenkins, David Castle, Jane Bailey, and Gareth Bailey.

Harvest festival at Crwys Road Baptist Church, *c.* 1967.

Four
Celebrations

Cranbrook Street VJ Day tea party, 1945.

Cranbrook Street VE Day party, 1945.

Cranbrook Street VE Day party, 8 May 1945.

Cranbrook Street, VE Day party, 8 May 1945.

Cairns Street celebrates King George V's Silver Jubilee in 1935. Not long after this picture was taken the notorious Cairns Street became Rhymney Street. This came about after 184 residents of Cairns Street petitioned the local authority to have the name changed. Emrys Davies, who was born in Cairns Street, recalled: '*It was notorious for being a very rough street and was nicknamed "Flagon Alley."*' The little boy second from the right in the front is Vic Wheeler who has lived in Rhymney Street all his life.

Standing outside the general stores at No. 35 Cairns Street are Mrs Ethel Goodall, Billy Fisher, Wilf Goodall, Lily Goodall, and Ruth Fisher. The lady to the right of the picture holding a baby is Mrs Taylor.

The children of Laytonia Avenue and North Road celebrate the Coronation in 1953. The boy in the front row, on the extreme left of picture, is Bernard Plain who went on to run for Great Britain.

The Coronation party in Laytonia Avenue was held in one of the garages there.

Celebrating the Coronation in 1953 with
a tea party are these children from
Coburn Street.

The two Mrs Mops in the Coburn Street Coronation fancy-dress competition are John Esposty (left) and Tommy Stone (right).

This golly, Gillian Goodall, won first prize in the fancy-dress competition. The names of Miss Britannia and the clown, who finished second and third respectively remain a mystery.

Residents of Thesiger Street gather to celebrate the coronation of King George VI and Queen Elizabeth in 1937. They are pictured above outside the corner grocery shop. Later, the shop was run by Miss Matilda Wakeham and was popularly known as 'Tilly's'.

VE Day street party in Thesiger Street, Cathays.

VE Day street party, Thesiger Street, 1945.

Coronation street party in Thesiger Street, 1953.

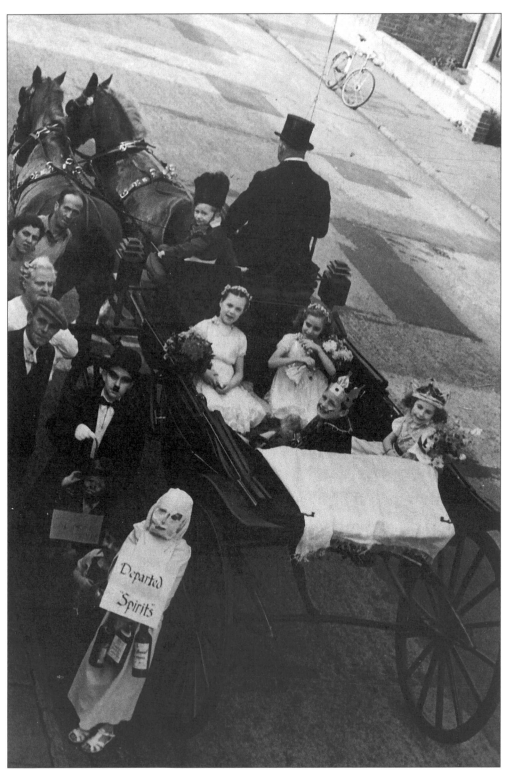

Wyeverne Road's Coronation party, 1953.

Wyeverne Road's Coronation party, 1953. From left to right: Ann Jenkins, -?-, Elaine Edmunds, Christine Jones, Bob Jackson, ? Jackson (Bob's younger brother).

VE Day celebrations in Little Wyeverne Road, May 1945. *'I was only nine years of age but I can remember the war. I was living in No. 36 Wyeverne Road, Cathays. We went to the shelters when the sirens sounded and one night German aircraft came over and bombed Cardiff. They blew up the biggest part of Wyeverne Road and Rhymney Street. There was one big family living at the end of Wyeverne Road and they all got killed by landmines.'* [Fred Nowell, in a letter to the *South Wales Echo* in 1997]. It was at No 19 Wyeverne Road that Mr and Mrs Palmer and their eight children were all killed after a parachute mine landed within a few yards of the Anderson air-raid shelter.

A Cathays Conservative Club outing, *c.* 1956.

The year is 1936 and these ladies belonging to the Cathays Conservative Club pose for a group picture before setting off on their day trip.

Residents of Flora Street and Cathays Terrace take part in VE Day celebrations, 1945.

VE day celebrations in Cathays Terrace, 1945. The cyclist is Fred Chedzoy, landlord of the Flora Hotel, and the tramp is none other than local butcher Jack Smith. *'On a night in January 1941, the German bombers dropped landmines on the bottom of Cathays Terrace, destroying houses and the Gospel Hall and the Baptist Church next door to our house. There were many people killed, I'm not sure how many... it was very frightening.'* [Jeanne Hoare, in a letter to the *South Wales Echo* in 1997]

Cathays Terrace residents put on a tea party for the Queen's coronation in 1953.

Coronation street party in Cathays Terrace, 1953.

Coronation party celebrations in Dalton Street, 1953.

Dalton Street VE Day celebrations. The little girl is Jackie Bryant who lived at No. 37 Dalton Street and who later became the author's wife. Her mother, Gladys Bryant, is seated second left.

Members of the Dalton Street Day Centre get in the mood before boarding the coach for a trip to Weston-super-Mare in 1976.

Monthermer Road senior citizens pictured before a day trip in 1968.

Schoolchildren from St Monica's gathered on the corner of Llantrisant Street and Hirwain Street to pose for this picture taken on the day of King George V and Queen Mary's Silver Jubilee in 1935.

Residents of Lisvane Street pose for this VE Day picture. The brothers Hugh, Reginald and Percy Cudlipp, who all became famed newspaper editors, came originally from Lisvane Street.

Mynachdy Road residents and children celebrating VE Day. The little girl on the extreme left is Wendy Whitfield (née Thompson); she is being held by her godmother, Mrs Irene Leyshon.

VJ Day, 15 August 1945, and Mynachdy Road neighbours pose for this picture.

A Coronation day party in Mynachdy Road, 1953.

Jeanette Delve, who lived at No. 86 Mynachdy Road, was voted floral queen at the 1952 Mynachdy Festival carnival. She sadly died two years later at the tender age of sixteen.

VE Day party in Robert Street. Mrs Kate Parfitt (Harry Parfitt's wife) is pictured seated on the extreme right.

Allensbank Road Coronation Day celebrations, 1953.

VE Day celebrations in Allensbank Road, May 1945.

Coronation Day celebrations in Allensbank Road, 1945.

Children from Allensbank Road School pose for a group photograph at the end of the Second World War.

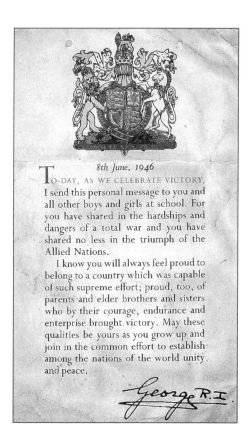

Personal message from the King that was given to all schoolchildren on the first anniversary of the War in Europe.

8th June, 1946

TO-DAY, AS WE CELEBRATE VICTORY, I send this personal message to you and all other boys and girls at school. For you have shared in the hardships and dangers of a total war and you have shared no less in the triumph of the Allied Nations.

I know you will always feel proud to belong to a country which was capable of such supreme effort; proud, too, of parents and elder brothers and sisters who by their courage, endurance and enterprise brought victory. May these qualities be yours as you grow up and join in the common effort to establish among the nations of the world unity and peace.

George R.I.

VE Day celebrations at Allensbank Road, May 1945.

Five

Sports and Entertainment

The notorious Maindy Pool where a number of adults and children were drowned, 1928.

The 1951 Glamorgan School Championships were the first athletics meet to be held at the new Maindy Stadium. *'The story had spread that the firm "En Tout Cas", who laid all the country's best cinder tracks, were going to lay the new Cardiff track, the only one in Wales at that time. But on my first visit I found that the track was no more than dust from Cardiff brickworks, a bright orange colour. It was like running on Barry Island sands. Nobody in Wales could, at first, run anything better than a 5-minute mile. However, by constantly rolling the brick dust, the surface improved although it was eight years before a bona fide track was laid. The track for the Empire Games at Cardiff Arms Park was ripped up the same night of the last day of the games, a Saturday. The press and media generally went mad, and so did a lot of other people, runners in Wales, in particular. But the Arms Park track was transported to Maindy, where it was relaid.'* [Bernard Baldwin MBE]

A tractor clears the site for construction of the Maindy Stadium terraces. Stones were taken from the Glamorgan Canal banks to be used on the site.

Workmen making good progress at Maindy Stadium.

The workmen are shown turfing the inside of an arena which was to stage numerous sporting events in athletics, rugby, and soccer. The author saw the legendary Welsh boxer Tommy Farr fight at the stadium in 1953.

Workmen laying the running track. Cathays High School can be seen in the background, to the right of picture.

A sectional view of the completed stadium which was to become the headquarters of Roath (Cardiff) Harriers, one of the oldest athletics clubs in the country.

Cycling takes place at Maindy Stadium for the first time and attracts a bumper crowd. The cycling track was one of the best in the world at the time and the famed Reg Harris raced there in 1951.

John Tarrant of Salford Harriers breaks the world 40-mile record at Maindy Stadium in November 1966. He clocked 4 hrs, 3 mins, 28 seconds, clipping 40 seconds off the record set by Alan Phillips (Norfolk Gazelles). Only an hour before the start, the track was under water after 24 hours of torrential rain. Miraculously it cleared, although the surface was left soft and difficult for the runners. Tarrant, who had the heart of a lion, sadly died a few years later with cancer. The man with the loudhailer is Bernard Baldwin MBE who organised the race.

Tommy Wood leads Rhys Davies, Ron Franklyn, Ken Flowers, and Brian Lee in the 1958 Welsh AAA marathon which started and finished at Maindy Stadium. Davies, who had won the 1957 race, won in a time of 2 hours 35 minutes 29 seconds. He won it for a third time in 1959.

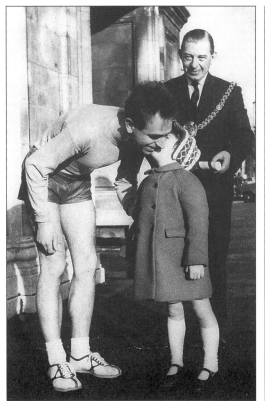 

Left: The Lord Mayor Alderman W.J. Hartland looks on as Brian Lee receives a kiss from his daughter Amanda before running to Mountain Ash with a New Year's (Nos Galan) message for the Chairman of the Mountain Ash Urban District Council, 1964. *Right*: Roath Harrier Malcolm Beames carries on the tradition two years later in 1966.

Cathays Conservative Club football team and members, *c.* 1948.

Cathays Conservative Club skittle team, 1921, winners of the Cardiff Conservative Club Championship (the Gronow Cup) and the Cardiff and District United Clubs' Championship A (Smith-Petersen Shield) and B (Freedom and Reform Shield) divisions.

Cathays Wednesdays AFC, winners of the J. Ingram Rees Challenge Cup, 1919/20 season. From left to right, back row: P.L. Williams (committee), H. Rose, E. Dart, D.J. Horne, N. Beazley (vice-captain), H.G. Harvey, W. Rumbelow, E.C. Greenfield (committee), D. Cosslett; middle row (sitting): A. Jones (committee), T. Harrison, A. Stephens, R.F. Cox (captain), P.J. Henry, J. Radford (captain, 2nd XI), J.A. Cosslett (hon. secretary and treasurer); front row: W.A. Carter, A.E. Horne, G. Tanner.

Cathays Wednesdays AFC, winners of both the Lord Ninian Cup and Ingram Rees Cup, and runners up in the first division of the Cardiff and District Wednesday Amateur Association Football League, 1924/25 season. From left to right, back row: W. Pearce (hon. treasurer), J.A. Cosslett (hon. secretary), Miss J. Dorward (committee), A. Jones (committee), W. Taber (vice-chairman); middle row: G. Badman, J. Sullivan, W. Benjamin, T. Green, F. Rice, A. Grant, H. Badman, W.A. Donovan, W. Jones (assistant hon. secretary); seated: B. Moore, W.W. Elson (vice-captain, 1st XI), W. Badman (captain, 1st XI), F. Ascott-Evans (chairman), J. Smith (captain, 2nd XI), I. Phillips (vice-captain, 2nd XI), B.P. Gwyther; on ground: W.A. Carter, A.C. Collier.

St Joseph's RC School rugby team, 1929/30 season. This team is believed to be the first ever fielded by the school. From left to right, back row: J. Cullen (trainer), T. Durston, T. Mead, W. Bartlett, P. Fitzgerald, J. Callan, J. Smith, J. Collins, J. Welsh; middle row: J. Harris, J. Pengelly, R. Freemantle, Father Ottway, D. Roche (captain), Father King, W. Cody, W. Bibey, C. Davies; seated: H. McLean, E. Sullivan, T. Collins, R. Lewis.

Cathays Amateur Boxing Club members
show off their trophies, c. 1933. Harry Parfitt,
who ran the club, is behind the boy with the
display case.

Cathays Boxing Club summer camp at
Nottage, Porthcawl, 1936. Harry Parfitt is
seen wearing spectacles.

Isobel and Frank Inker are pictured here with the FA Cup won by Cardiff City in 1927, after they overcame Arsenal 1–0 at Wembley. Isobel played for Willows Aircraft AFC which later became Cardiff City Ladies AFC. Ladies' football thrived nationally in the 1920s, later going into a long period of decline before its resurgence in recent years.

These Coburn Street ladies celebrated the Coronation in 1953 by playing a game of soccer. From left to right, back row: Bert Miller, Mrs Singleton, Kitty Hooper, Barbara Esposty, Lena Moyle, Joan Goodall, George Oliver; front row: Jean Miller, Maria Retter, Rose Wakeham, Mrs Coates, Margaret Miller.

Cardiff City Supporters Club AFC, Cardiff and District Football League division two winners. From left to right, back row: E. Griffiths, P. Bowers, T. Brown, T. Burnell, D. Jones, G. Williams, C. Casseldine, B. O'Mara, D. England, D. Davies, R. Knowles; front row: George Reed, D. McGill, M. Davies, B. Morgan, J. Thomas. The little girl in the picture is Janet Davies, daughter of Denny Davies.

Third left (front row) is Lee Beames from Gabalfa. A member of the Western *Mail & Echo* team which won the business house relays at Sophia Gardens in 1982. His father Mac Beames is shown on the extreme right.

The Gower Hotel darts team which won the Champion of Champions competition in 1972. From left to right: J. O'Leary, Alan Jones, George Parsons, -?-, Viv Parfitt, T. Reynolds, Peter Bridger, Harold Dring, Phil Lane, Glyn Parfitt, Peter Fisher, Larnie Jones, and Jim Mace (a well-known barber who had a shop in Crwys Road).

Carol Smith and Shelia Bates, two outstanding roller-skating stars of the 1950s, seen here at the Embassy Skating Rink in Cathays Terrace, which closed in 1969.

The Plaza Cinema opened in March 1928 and was closed in October 1981. It was demolished in July 1985 and the site, once occupied by an old farmhouse, is now filled by the Meridian Court retirement homes.

The Regal Dance Hall in Western Avenue was a popular venue for thousands of Cardiffians in the 1950s and 1960s. *'The Regal was where the flyover is now. Ken Ellerway had a small band and played there. It was a meeting place for everyone. A quick game of snooker and then off to the Plaza'.* (Owen Martin)

The Coronet Cinema in Woodville Road was popularly known as the 'Cora' and more often than not as 'the Bug House'. The last film show was in 1958 and the building was demolished in 1973 to make way for Superfine Garage. A block of flats now stands on the site. The author's sister, Valerie, taught him to tell the time by the illuminated clock in the cinema.

Six

Events

The Bryant brothers in Cathays Cemetery, *c.* 1912. Bill Bryant is the boy in the middle.

Crwys Hall Sunday school outing to Draethen, *c.* 1912.

Soldiers take a break from entertaining the local children to pose for this picture in Maindy Barracks fields, 1904. The tops of the shops in Whitchurch Road can be seen in the background.

The funeral in Cathays Cemetery of Sergeant Observer Arthur Page who was killed in a flying accident in 1919. He is believed to have lived in Flora Street.

Left: William and Minnie Jones of Coburn Street, who were married during the First World War. *Right:* following in their father's footsteps, daughter Gladys Jones joined the ATS and her brother William served in the Army Medical Corps during the Second World War. *'I will never forget the night we were bombed. The house just collapsed around us. We had to climb over the rubble to get out. I was under the table and my mother and baby brother Robert were sheltering in the pantry, as we didn't have an air-raid shelter. The bomb fell three doors away killing little Margaret Davies and her brother Edgar.'* [Mrs Joan Burnell (née Goodall), who lived at No. 36 Coburn Street]

Peter Clifton of St Mark's Avenue, who was based at Maindy Barracks, is presented by Sir Cennydd Traherne with the Lord Lieutenant's Award for recognition of outstanding service and devotion to duty with the Territorial Army Volunteer Reserve in 1975.

March past of ARPs at Maindy Pool, c. 1944. The lady in the group of three (centre) is Mrs Nancy Pitman. The houses in Gelligaer Street can be seen in the background.

27th (Cardiff) Girls' Training Corps at Maindy, 1945. They paraded at Allensbank School. '*The lane running between Maindy Barracks field and the Bowling Green/Cathays High School was referred to as 'the Burma Road', it being a significant comparison with the real Burma Road convoys of Allied lorries trundling through South-east Asia during the Second World War. While the Americans were at Maindy, we lads used to walk the length of the lane, from Gelligaer Street to New Zealand Road, asking the Yanks for gum or sweets and promising to bring our 'imaginary' older sisters along next time! In fact, the women who did spend time with them were considered of a doubtful character to say the least,…*' [Alun Williams]

Before the First World War, No. 47 Dalton Street, Cathays was an army recruitment office. The little girl in this picture (c. 1910) is Gladys Redwood and the sign on the plaque reads: 'National Association Employment Reserve Soldiers Office'. Holding her hand is her brother, William, who served in the Army Service Corps during the First World War.

Left: 'Digging for Victory' – Billy Lee (the author's father) on leave with his daughter Valerie alongside him. *Right*: same girl, different hairstyle! Valerie Lee is seen here in front of the Anderson air-raid shelter in which she spent many sleepless nights with her mother and brother, *c.* 1945.

Left: Bill Bryant, of Dalton Street, holds his baby daughter Jacqueline in the garden, 1940. *Right*: Mr Bryant, standing in almost the same spot twenty years later in 1960, is pictured nursing his granddaughter Amanda (Jacqueline's daughter). Both mother and daughter were born in No. 37 Dalton Street.

The author, Brian Lee (left), is pictured in the garden of his house at No. 23 Thesiger Street, c. 1949, with his friend, Keith Parkins, who later became a well-known ballroom dancer who appeared on television regularly in the 1960s.

Sisters Beryl and Edna Davey of Thesiger Street, wearing their Capitol Cinema usherette uniforms, c. 1952. Their paternal grandmother, Emily Davey, who lived in Woodville Road was a Blackfoot Indian and she lived to 103 or 104 and died around 1954. Her husband, William, had been an Indian scout.

Bill Stamp is on accordion and Bill Bryant
is on drums. The pianist is Arthur
Haslam. This trio played at weddings and
other social occasions in the 1940s.

Cardiff entertainer Stan Stennett seen
here in the 1950s. He lived for a short
while in Talygarn Street.

Left: standing in the middle of Dalton Street is Fred Bryant (Bill Bryant's brother), the Cathays cartoonist whose work was praised by Walt Disney. The Melbourne Café, which used to be in Crwys Road, can just be seen in the rear of the picture. *Right and below*: one of the municipal-election leaflets drawn by Fred Bryant in the 1960s.

Gabalfa residents deep in discussion over plans for a new park, *c.* 1969. They are Councillor Parry, Mrs Winifred Hilliard, Mrs Kathleen Jones and Vera Hutchings. The five acre site was adjacent to the Gabalfa interchange and fronting Celtic Road.

It is Cardiff University rag week, *c.* 1950 and Harry Parfitt and his horse and cart wait outside the Welsh Office for the start of the parade.

The sign on Harry Parfitt's pony and trap is obscured, but it could be inviting the Cardiff ratepayers to 'Vote for Jenkins!' (c. 1953).

Viscount Tonypandy (George Thomas) signs 100 souvenir cover envelopes at the Woodville Road headquarters in readiness for the centenary day of the Boys' Brigade, 1993. Looking on are Captain Allen Hambly (left) and David Dwyer of the 22nd Cardiff company.

St Cyprian's Dramatic Society, 1932.

St Mark's Church demonstration, 29 June 1912.

On 20 February 1950 the last tram made its final journey on the Whitchurch Road route.

The taller of these two uniformed figures is John Wakeling who drove the last Cardiff tram, seen here in Whitchurch Road, 1950. To the left of the picture can be seen St Mark's Church Institute.

Residents of Cairns Street (later renamed Rhymney Street) before setting out on a day trip to Barry Island. The lady on the extreme left of the picture is Mrs Kate Parfitt seen holding her son Billy, *c.* 1920.

Thesiger Street outing, *c.* 1920. The lady sitting in the coach (third from the right) is Mrs Sarah Driscoll, who lived at No. 9 Thesiger Street.

After heavy rain in 1960, the River Taff burst its banks flooding most of the Gabalfa housing estate.

Seven
Places and People

Llys Tal-y-Bont farmhouse, 1890. The noted Welsh historian Professor William Rees claimed that Llys Tal-y-Bont ('the Court at the Head of the Bridge') was 'the last link with much ancient Welsh history'.

Harleys Farm, Allensbank, c. 1890. This gave Allensbank Road its name and the farm was situated on the west side of the road at the entrance to Inglefield Avenue.

Crwys House on the corner of Woodville Road/Crwys Road, June 1982. The Woodville Road Baptist Church can be seen on the right of the picture.

Llys Tal-y-Bont. *'On the eastern bank of the Glamorganshire Canal, where the canal approaches within about a hundred yards of the Taff, stands a rambling thatched farmhouse popularly known as Lislabont or Islabont.'* [John Hobson Matthews, *Cardiff Records*]

Grange Farm, Llantrissant Street, 1890. It was situated at the west end of Llantrisant Street and demolished in 1899. William Davies is believed to have been the last tenant.

The Lodge, Blackweir, 1971. Roath (Cardiff) Harriers used to start their cross-country runs from the Lodge in the 1950s and 1960s.

St Andrew and St Teilo Church Hall, Wyeverne Road, Cathays, 1957.

St Andrew's Institute, Wyeverne Road. It was opened by Lord Tredegar, c. 1900

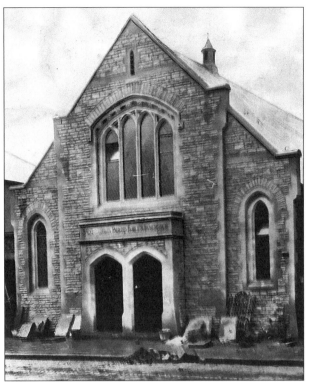

A print of the Welsh Calvinistic Church on Crwys Road. The architect was John H. Phillips of Cardiff. The church floor could accommodate six hundred worshippers and it was built by Harry Gibbon, of Cardiff, at a cost of £2,660. It is now a mosque.

St Mark's Church, Whitchurch Road. It was demolished in September 1968 to make way for the flyover.

St Mark's Church, Whitchurch Road, December 1966.

Crwys Road/Cathays Terrace, 1891.

The Taff Vale Railway offices, Salisbury Road, Cathays, 1972, Formerly the site of Biggs Brewery

Allensbank Road after the last air-raid on Cardiff in 1943.

Mr Hopkins's house, situated near Cathays Cemetery, 1890.

Cathays Cemetery Chapel. It was demolished in 1986.

Cathays Cemetery. This was opened in 1859. The legendary Cardiff boxer, 'Peerless' Jim Driscoll, is buried there, c. 1905.

The first photographic memorial to be placed in Cathays Cemetery. It was erected in the memory of the children of S. Aitken Esq; and reads '1879 Winnie died December 10 aged 4 Claud died December 22 aged 3. Thy Loving Kindness Is Better Than Life.'

Flowering Sunday in Cathays Cemetery, *c.* 1890.

The superintendent's office at Cathays Cemetery. During the Second World War a landmine and several bombs destroyed hundreds of graves, c. 1905.

Bala Road, Gabalfa, c. 1950.

Gabalfa interchange, North East side, December 1972.

Whitchurch Road junction, October 1967.

Whitchurch Road junction, 1967. St Mark's Church is still standing.

North Road/Whitchurch Road, 1967, just before the houses were demolished.

Western Avenue, 1967. *'When Western Avenue was built in the late 1920s we went to the River Bridge to witness Alderman Hill Snook declare the bridge open. There was a wide blue ribbon across the bridge and when he cut it all us kids cheered.'* [Joan Taylor]

Construction of Eastern Avenue, 1969.

Construction of Eastern Avenue, 1969

Cathays Terrace/Catherine Street, 1977. A popular figure who lived in Catherine Street during the 1950's was Ralph Thomas the street bookmaker. His most famous punter was a young Arab lad who starred in the film *Lawrence of Arabia*. In the film he died in a quicksand.

The Glamorgan County Hall, Cathays Park, *c.* 1948. As a boy the author played on the Albert Hodge statues which symbolise navigation and mining. County Hall was opened in 1912.

The presentation to the City of Cardiff of a German gun captured at Loos by the Welsh Guards, 18 November 1915.

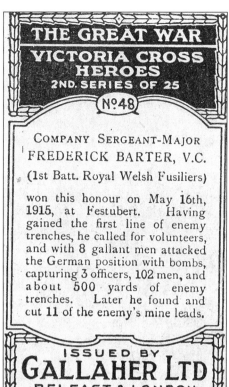

THE GREAT WAR
VICTORIA CROSS
HEROES
2ND. SERIES OF 25
Nº 48

COMPANY SERGEANT-MAJOR
FREDERICK BARTER, V.C.
(1st Batt. Royal Welsh Fusiliers)

won this honour on May 16th, 1915, at Festubert. Having gained the first line of enemy trenches, he called for volunteers, and with 8 gallant men attacked the German position with bombs, capturing 3 officers, 102 men, and about 500 yards of enemy trenches. Later he found and cut 11 of the enemy's mine leads.

ISSUED BY
GALLAHER LTD
BELFAST & LONDON

Left: Fred Barter VC of Cathays was awarded this the highest military distinction while serving in the Royal Welsh Fusiliers during the First World War. *Right*: the cigarette-card eulogy to Fred Barter.

No. 60 Daniel Street, (middle) Cathays, the birthplace of Fred Barter. The author has campaigned in the local press for a commemorative plaque to be placed on the house.

Dennis Lloyd outside the Embassy Social Club in Cathays Terrace. Until it closed in 1969, the building was known as the Embassy Skating Rink.

Battalion Church parade to Cathays Methodist Church in 1961. The 23rd Cardiff Company is led here by Capt. W.H. Miller. The Lord Mayor, Alderman E. Ewart Pearce, takes the salute, watched by members of the City Council. S. Tapper Jones, Town Clerk, is next to the Lord Mayor.

Battalion Church Parade to Cathays Methodist Church in 1961. 23rd Cardiff Company led by W.H.Miller, Capt. at the March Past.   The Lord Mayor, Alderman E.Ewar Pearce taking the salute watched by members of the City Council. S.Tapper Jones,Town Clerk next to Lord Mayor

Eight
Special Occasions

King George V and Queen Mary at the University of Wales, Cathays Park, 25 June 1912, during the royal visit to Cardiff in which they laid the foundation stone of the National Museum of Wales.

Tom Waley and Bob Goodall passing through Wyeverne Road during the Cardiff City Social Club fancy-dress walk, *c.* 1955.

Children from St Joseph's Roman Catholic School taking part in the Corpus Christi procession, Park Place, *c.* 1970.

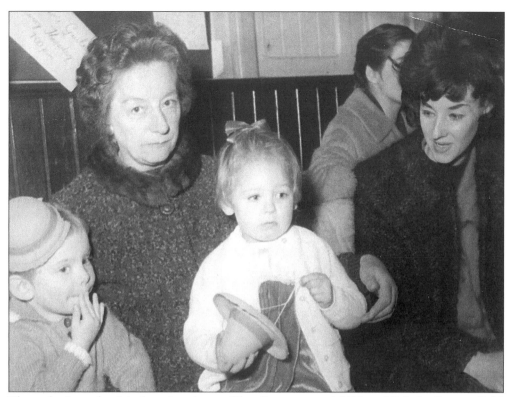

The author's mother Mrs Joan Lee shows off her first two grandchildren, Nicholas Beames (left) and Amanda Lee (right) at the *Western Mail & Echo* Christmas Party in the Cathays Methodist Church Hall, *c.* 1962.

The Embassy Skating Rink staged a Christmas party for these children in 1956.

The christening of Gail Creed at St Andrew's and St Teilo's Church, Woodville Road, 1955. From left to right: Jack Smith, Millie Smith, Pat Creed, Millie Creed, Doreen Creed, Violet Cooper (godmother), Carol Smith, and Ron Creed.

Wedding group outside the Flora Hotel in 1956. The happy couple are Val Williams and David Croot. The girl on the extreme right of the picture is Hazel Williams, later to become Miss Wales.

Lily Taylor, (centre front row) later Mrs Latham, of Woodville Road, celebrates her twentieth birthday on 11 April 1912.

The Taylors of Cathays line up for a family portrait, c. 1922. From left to right: Beatrice (Ash), Gladys (Bryant), Lawrence, Minnie (Stamp), and Lily (Latham).

Seen celebrating the fortieth (ruby) wedding anniversary of their mother and father, Elvira and Albert Evans, in April 1953, are, from left to right: Cissie Cooper (who ran the popular fish and chip shop in Coburn Street), her husband Gus, her sister Mabel (who had the draper's shop next door), and Cissie's other sister Margaret. *'Just after the war there were plenty of shops in Coburn Street, these included Cissie Evans's the fish and chip shop, Jones the cobbler, Abelson's the optician, Charlie Bensen the barber, Hurford the grocer and Hemming's sweetshop. The pub on the corner of Wyeverne Road, now called the New Ely, was then known as the Coburn.'* [Mrs Joan Burnell (née Goodall)]

Albert and Elvira Evans cut their ruby wedding anniversary cake in their Coburn Street home.